Class

Best Wishes

Dick W. Rother

aka P. U. Ravour

MURMURINGS
of the HEART

P. A. Ramour

iUniverse, Inc.
Bloomington

Murmurings of the Heart

Copyright © 2012 P. A. Ramour

iUniverse books may be ordered through booksellers or by contacting:

iUniverse
1663 Liberty Drive
Bloomington, IN 47403
www.iuniverse.com
1-800-Authors (1-800-288-4677)

ISBN: 978-1-4759-5792-1 (sc)
ISBN: 978-1-4759-5794-5 (hc)
ISBN: 978-1-4759-5793-8 (e)

Library of Congress Control Number: 2012920028

Printed in the United States of America

iUniverse rev. date: 11/16/2012

This book is dedicated to a foxy lady whom I call Angel.
She brought a new kind of love to me in my golden years,
the phase of life when most are settled in life's routines.

I Search the Stars

I search the stars for an answer to a question I can't even state.
How can the stars even transfer their message to me or relate?
From where will my enlightenment come?
Shall I inquire beyond the unknown?
There is an underlying urge of excitement.
I'm in want for my curiosity to be shown.
I know there is more than what is apparent.
To understand fully is elusive.
My inquisitiveness may seem errant.
I know all that's seen is inconclusive.

Where Have All the Flowers Gone?

My heart is telling me yet
to write this epithet
of a love passed in a season.
In its time for its reason:
Skoal!

O! How I shall now lament
of a love and time which has spent
its desires and dreams,
just to be rent from my soul.

As leaves in autumn fall to die,
my memories of our joys do cry.
Our season to love has passed on by.
It is winter in June, and I hear the bell toll.

Do you cast away a love song so true
only because it's no longer new?
Or do you feel its song is trying?
Where are the tears?
Should I be crying?
Cajole!

A conquest, you said was I, touché.
A love found I.
Olé!
Look at me now this day.
My heart is rent right from my soul.

Again I'm reminded to lock my heart.
Shall ever I unlock it again and start
its exodus to the Promised Land?

Behold!
Where is my heart?
Has it turned cold?

I Must Go Now

So now it's time for us to part,
although it is heavy on my heart.
We've tried and plied our differences deep.
We've cried, too oftentimes, ourselves to sleep.
So I must go now.

What you and I have been longing for
is our love returned, as once before.
Now it's just a fantasy.

Oh, how I've yearned to know again
the joy we had another time when
our love was new,
our love was true.
I worshiped you.
So I must go now.

No more to hear you call my name,
first, with love and then disdain.
No longer a need to reason why
we're unable to see eye to eye,
or even try.
And so, I must go now.
Good-bye.

Soar Like an Eagle

Like a mother eagle with chicks in her high nest
searching woodland and shore from East to West,
her need before her, chicks hunger behind her,
with outstretched wings carrying her
from her love, for her love.
Like the eagle my heart has risen from its brambly nest
to soar, to feel the wind on my breast.
I have sought pleasure these passing years,
even to this day.
Pleasure will not abide with fear.
Together they will not stay.
Although pleasure will mix with tears,
why are we made this way?
In cloudy days and chilly nights
or balmy weather with sun so bright,
I pursued pleasure and her daughters
across far lands and across broad waters.
It was the least of my delight
to pursue pleasure and gather treasure day and night.
Now I can only measure one meritorious plight:
to know love and how it was meant to be given,
not in measure, not in time, but in living.

The Carousel of Life

When the carousel of life its spinning slows,
and the calliope's rhythm wanes in the glow,
lights are flickering while the stallions bow.
The world is passing
like a stream's bubbling flow
on the carousel.
You wish for another turn around.
Too soon it's time to step down.
The horse you chose was a mighty steed.
You climbed in the saddle with such confident speed,
knowing you'd be carried to that oasis you desired.
Within your heart all emotions were fired.
The music in palpitating rhythm played
while the steed you rode in cadence stayed.
You looked for that familiar face as you spun,
seeking to be seen by a loved dear one.
But too fast you went to see things clear.
The face you sought just wasn't near.
So as the carousel ride came to its end,
you left its fantasy in search of your friend.
And soon enough you found the one whom you sought,
in searching from a horse by the ticket you bought
on life's carousel.
It was then so late that you realized
you can't see your friend when you're mesmerized
by bugles and horns and timpani.
When you're spinning on your horse, you're in such frenzy.
So you get off your horse, put your feet on the ground,
stop riding a fantasy, a true friend you've found.
She was waiting for you to finish your ride
on the carousel.

September

In the evening calm of late summer
tree shadows silently invade the meadow,
its verdant summer green waning to autumn amber.
The setting harvest sun paints the layered clouds
like an iridescent kaleidoscope with shades of lavender
distilled to orange, then to magenta,
giving all nature a golden sheen,
plaited with the Master's hand.
It's late September.
Listen!
A grosbeak's song from the grassy sedge.
There is a deer grazing beneath the choke cherry hedge.
The wood duck whistles from deep in the thicket.
Urgings of autumn,
Slow chirps the cricket,
as the descending chill announces the summer's departing.
Silky curtains of mist like eiderdown rise above
the marsh beyond the meadow.
Where a resident bittern voices a lonesome call,
with its kerchunk, kerchunk, kerchunk!
I know this autumn holiday is calling.

Yes, calling the winter back to make the waters still,
back to cover the warmth of Mother Earth
beneath a protective blanket of snow.
Even though the shortening days are yet sunny and warm,
the fall rains bring their cooling patter
with a sudden chill.
But for those who dwell in Earth's fertile garden,
it doesn't matter.
It's only right
that Mother Earth should also delight
in rest.
I'm blessed.
My heart is silent now in reverence,
knowing that summer has past.
Thankful for the season,
and how it has its spell cast
with whispering leaves.
The rustling of the wind through the corn sheaves
and the sweet laughter of a bubbling brook
savor the earthy aroma of newly mown hay
with stars reflecting on a moonlit bay.
And now it's September.
It is summer's end.

Evening at Ada Lake

Not a whisper of an evening breeze,
mere enough to tickle the autumn leaves.
The harvest moon lifting from behind the tall pines;
in unison, like waltzing, the descending sun shines.
A glorious exit of colors enhanced by the clouds
too soon to be enveloped in darkened shrouds.
Moon shadows of trees on the lake smooth as glass,
reflections of stars for His namesake, alas.
To be carried away in spirit by the likes of all this
needs to be shared with someone, such bliss.

I hear the coyotes their far lonesome call.
I hear a bear grumble as if to answer them all.
That wily raccoon by the water's edge,
washing his catch on a rocky ledge.

Why am I blessed with all this, this night?
Is it only to share with the owl so white?
It needs to be shared with someone like you,
who'll understand how it can renew
forgotten memories pushed away by time
of loved ones, dear ones, friendships sublime.

Lonesomeness can heighten the splendor of being.
I'm part of the earth, the sky, though time is fleeing.
If only God would again make the earth stand still
for moments like these and to know His will.
Come, share this with me.

Good Morning

Rolling thunder from lightning afar.
Insistent breezes.
The rain's tempo of pitter-patter increases.
Don't stop the rain!
A little while more let me dream.
A flash of light seen through eyes closed in reverie,
then distant rolling thunder calls my name.
Wake up!
Come see the pattering against the window pane.
Rain!
Wake up, the dancing raindrops call to me,
but my slumber is more favored toward unfinished dreams.
I will enjoy them both for now,
the rain and the dream.
They are companions somehow, they enhance each other—
slumber, dreams, the refrain of dancing drops of rain.

Plowing is done, planting is done,
firewood is stacked tight.
Painting to do, but that's all right
I'd like to get some fishing in too,
but for now, we need watering,
and for now I need slumbering.

As the soft glow of dawn entices the flowers to bloom,
an urging of restlessness nudges me from my room.
Open the window, ah! a pleasant chill of fresh-washed air.
I'm part of nature, a feeling too rare.
Blades of grass, flowers, trees, the cool of morn, rain.
The sun insisting the night shall wane.

From my window, till now unseen, a bluebird,
weaving through the glistening sheen of boughs and limbs.
From the edge of the woods to my lawn he dances and skims,
but Mr. Robin lives there, he's not willing to share
or say hello. He's too busy pulling up his breakfast.
Welcome to this day, sings the bluebird to me.

Listen to My Heart

Listen to my heart, while it's beating like this.
Listen to my heart, come closer to me.
Time is fleeting by while you're in my arms.
My heart is telling me, don't let go, you love her so.

You'll never know another love like this.
You've never felt such a tender kiss before like this.
Just listen to your heart.

If the sun should stand still once more,
it would stop just for the two of us.
To be like this forever more, I'm so sure of it.
Just listen to your heart
because
it is so rapidly beating with mine.
Can you feel it?
If my heart should burst will you heal it?
Come with me.
If you lead I will follow, yes, I will, darling.
Darling, can't you see I'm so helpless without you?
What do you feel when my arms are about you?

Darling, where this anxious heart will take me, I don't know!
What will this burning inside and yearnings lead us to?
Do you know?
Are you timid? Well, darling, I am too.
I tremble to think what this is leading us to.

What can we do, what can we do?
I can't stop, I can't stop. I'm losing control;
I'm giving you my soul.

Isn't that what you want me to do?
I confess, that's what I want to do.
Darling,
listen to my heart.
It's keeping time with yours.
If any closer to you I can be, I am lost.
Darling, I am lost, lost in your embrace.
Darling, don't let go, stay so close, so close to me.
Let me feel your beating heart next to mine.
Let your breath on my shoulder warm me all over.
Your touch tells me so much.
Listen to my heart.
Let me keep this moment forever to remember,
to remember this moment through all time,
your heart beating with mine.
I will not forget
how our hearts met.
I cannot forget
how our hearts met. How our hearts met.

Your Sweet Song

I love you so much, you're my dream.
I want you so much, and it seems
you'll always be near to me.
You'll always be dear to me,
You'll always be here for me.
That's how it should be.
And,
I love you so much, you're everything
that I need, dear, can't you see?
A love like ours is just meant to be.
It's meant to be for you and me
for wherever you go,
I want you to know
I love you so much, you're my dream.
It seems that I need your touch,
and there is no other such love as ours.
How can I ever show you my dream?
Come share this dream with me,
would you please?
Then you would surely know,
our love will grow and grow.
Please come with me,
so we can share this dream.
Then the whole world will see
just how true love can be.
Won't you say yes to me?
For our love is meant to be
through all eternity.

Though the sky, the land, the sea,
may pass away into time,
with love this sublime,
your heart with mine
will beat love's sweet rhyme.
Can't you see our love was meant to be?
I love you so much, don't ever go.
I love you so much, don't you know?
I would be lost without you,
lost, as a beacon of light in the fog and dew,
wandering from place to place,
searching for your lovely face.
I love you so much my darling,
don't ever go away,
for without your sweet love,
I languish through the day.
For all I do is dream of your sweet song.
You're on my mind all through the day,
and all night long, and, darling, you are my dream.
My dream can be a reality
if you would just say,
just sigh a sweet word to me.
Then the two of us would be as one,
one under the moon, the stars, the sun,
then the heavens would be ours.
You'll be mine and I'll be yours
forevermore.

We'll Work around It

When I was a boy it was my joy
to walk in the freshly turned dirt
while Dad was plowing.
With a "gee" or a "haw" and a slap of the reins,
those big sweaty horses would start bowing,
pushing in their harness, shiny with sweat,
frothy at their mouths and just as wet
as Dad while they labored in the field.
The earth breathed a fragrance as sweet as buttered rum
as its soul was exposed to the drying sun.
The smell of the horses was like a tonic too.
Dad would coax them on with his song of woo.
With a "gee" and a "haw" and an "easy now, boys,"
the plow sailed under the ground with a whistling noise.
I waded in the furrow as the sod rolled under,
waves of dirt covering my boots all around. In my wonder,
I didn't understand
how the freshly plowed land
could hatch new stones each year.
Was it planned?
Like newfound treasure, it was my pleasure
to pick each stone for mending the rock fence,
four feet high by measure.
When Dad would encounter a boulder stubbornly deep,
he would say "We'll work around her, let her sleep
until next year."
So I learned to work around things that won't budge.
If it doesn't cooperate with a gentle nudge,
I can leave it lay and walk away knowing
I can't carry that stone, can't carry a grudge.

15

The Meadow

Say au revoir, but, darling, do not say good-bye,
for my heart will stay right here with you.
It cannot leave, for you have captured it
so I shall never ever get it back again.
And I know
you'll take good care of it, for it's yours always.
Yes, it's yours to keep; it's all I can give.
It's the only way I can live, if you keep my heart.
Keep it with yours—the two beating together
will be so complete, oh so complete, you see,
and if
you keep my heart I know it will beat faithfully,
faithfully as the seasons come and go,
surely as the mountain snow melts in spring,
and into the stream the waters will flow
with sweetness that the flowers bring
to the meadow.
The meadow where first we met, my darling,
all the flowers were in bloom.
The dew was like diamonds on every glistening petal
and your sweet essence was intoxicating as perfume.

So when I go,
I will leave my heart with you.
I cannot keep it from you, dear.
I will keep the fragrance of your charms,
remembering the warmth of your loving arms.
Until I return, until we're together again
in the meadow
it will bloom again with the fragrance that's only ours.
Only we have known the wonders of these mountains high,
the splendor of the valley low, this special place of ours.
Here in the meadow,
the meadow with the meandering stream,
where you and I dreamed our dream.
It is ours alone and how we cherish it—
this time, this place, the moments divine.
You've captured my heart.
Don't say good-bye.
just say au revoir, dear heart.
For my soul aches when we're apart.
It aches for you alone,
and like the tide, I will come to you once more
in the meadow.

The Loveliness of Silence

No one's ever heard a butterfly—
it cannot speak nor sing,
it just hovers quietly around
and shows off its pretty wings.

Each tiny wing a masterpiece
of intricate design,
with hues that blend and complement,
so tranquil and refined.

And no one's ever heard a firefly
turn on its tiny light.
Without a click, it flips its switch,
and makes no noise in the night.

And there it is, in all its glory,
its wee light flashing off and on
until it disappears in silence,
along with moths across the lawn.

And what about white fleecy clouds
that aimlessly drift by?
They help us dream of things unseen,
though we can't hear them in the sky.

Like soft meringue, they peak and hang
soundlessly above the ground.
They tantalize our seeking eyes
as we watch in awe; they make no sound.

Puffs of smoke from chimney tops
come skipping through the air.
Gentle breezes make them dance,
what lovely visions there.

But we can't hear a puff of smoke,
nor can we hold it in our hands.

But we can watch it float away
silently across the land.
With the first snow of winter on the ground,
untouched, unmarked, pristine.
Lace like frost gathers on window panes
and crystal icicles that gleam.

Impressive beauties, each and every one,
that inspire men to whisper.
Do not disturb, but revere,
such a wondrous mixture.

A white full moon in a still dark night
with a host of silver stars.
Free to see and wish upon
and spend lovely, quiet hours.

In splendid stillness lies the night,
with peaceful beauty there.
Which forces one to bended knee,
in grateful, silent prayer.

To see a baby's smile or a sleeping child
or napping cat upon a lap.
So pleasurable and treasure immeasurable
are silent joys that entrap.

True, a picture's worth a thousand words,
though it never makes a sound.
It communicates in ways unheard,
and lasts forever and beyond.

It's the lovely, silent things we see
that our ears will never hear.
They speak softly to our listening hearts,
distinct, succinct, and clear.

We're grateful that God gave us ears
to hear His awesome sounds.
Yet the loveliness of silence
is wondrous when it is found.

Memories

When I was just a boy with Teddy Bear a-dragging,
With delight I pulled my sister Olive in our little red wagon.
One year older than I. I thought she was a queen,
To the store some candy to buy, and places in between.
Now Brother Ted, he was a tease, told me of witches and ghosts,
and if I should sneeze, the goblins would turn me into toast.
So, from the corner of my eye, I watched all the time
for creepy scary things when the sun went down about nine.

Grandma well understood her rowdy little bunch.
She fixed fried potatoes and beans every day for lunch.
With seven dirty faces but hands that were clean,
we all took our places, not to be heard but only to be seen.
Grandma had a thimble on her finger constantly.
She could evoke quite a howl with a snap so gingerly.

Brother Keith, the athlete had his friends, the "Stinky Six",
No one could stay ahead of all their crazy tricks.
They built model airplanes, sailed them from the barn roof high.
Some flew too far to chase so, little plane, good-bye.

The oldest brother Tom was an engineer so bright,
we respected his authority—if we didn't, there was a fight.
Big sister Ruth got married way to soon.
I hardly knew her, but when she left, I got her room.

Little brother George was his own in every way.
He never needed anyone when he was at his play.
I remember sitting on top of Josie, our Guernsey cow.
She gave us milk and friendship—I even miss her now.
From my perch I'd watch and listen as beside her Dad would bow,
and thought what a friend is that big old warm cow.

Chickens we had a-running so free in the yard,
they never would stray any further than the chard.
Mama tended the garden, showed us how to plant and weed.

We diligently obeyed her; we knew there was a need.
She had a willow stick pared down like a whip.
If Ma said to hoe, you didn't give her lip.
Picking berries was the most fun of all.
and what you didn't eat, you threw like a ball.
If you could run fast enough to escape that wicked willow branch,
Grandma would eventually corner you in the kitchen and make you dance
with another menacing willow whip in her hand.
We used to see who could step the highest,
shout the loudest, and laugh the longest.
We'd stop our antics in fear when we'd hear
heavy footsteps on the porch and Dad would appear.

Dad's gentle hand you see was calloused and had such girth.
It was never raised in anger but with authority and worth,
it always seemed a danger to ever question why
it could be so intimidating, though he wouldn't hurt a fly.

With seven adventurous children, Mom had no time to spare,
except at bedtime, in her creaky rocking chair.
She'd rock and sing the youngest to sleep in her lap each night.
The song I will always remember is kept in my heart all right.

Mom would sing

Good night, my someone; goodnight, my love.
Sleep tight, my someone; sleep tight, my love.
Our star is shining its brightest light,
so goodnight, my someone, goodnight.
Sweet dreams, my someone, if sleep there be.
Sweet dreams to carry you close to me.
I wish they may, and I wish they might.
Now good night, my someone, good night.

I think of our dog named Jim and of Fang the cat so fertile.
We had frogs and snakes, pet mice and even a turtle,
a feather bed for sleeping and a washtub for baths,
we snapped wet towels on bare behinds just for laughs.
These times are gone, long since have they past,
but these growing pains surely will forever last
in my memory.

Over the Hill

Well, good morning, old friend, nice of you to stop by.
I was just recalling that day back when—it was in July.
Remember the day? It was sort of like this, hot and muggy.
You stopped that runaway horse from tearing up the buggy.
If it hadn't been for you there, coming astride,
it would have been for Sis and me our last ride.
You always seem to come around just at a time,
a time when I have a need for an extra hand.

What is it now that brings you to my door?
I'm not in want like I have been before.
Most everything is like it should be, I guess.
In my heart I know there could be less
commotion and fussing, if some would give it a rest.
What's that you say? I'm not sure I heard you right.
It wouldn't be any other way no matter how hard I fight?
Well, I guess you know, I don't take kindly to feuding and fighting.
It just ain't right.

I'd rather walk over the hill behind my home,
sit under an old oak tree and let my mind roam.
It can roll around in the meadow of my dreams,
and I can get to the bottom of all my foolish schemes
beneath that old oak tree.

This patch of woods behind my place is the oldest in the state.
Never been an axe to it, or burned, as recorded to this date.
I cleared a spot just big enough for this house that I built.
I didn't want to disturb the groundcover you see—
it is nature's quilt.

Now this here linden tree will blossom soon and smell so sweet
and fill every room with the best your nose will ever meet.
Now come around in back with me, toward the hill behind.
I want to show you something that will be stirring to your mind.

Okay, now look real good, do you see through the wood?
See that choke cherry tree, guarding my yard, look hard.
She's home and haven to the birds day and night.
Except when Ollie the Owl decides to light
in her arms,
and whispers *who, who* by the moonlight.

Folks say it's the biggest choke cherry tree ever grown to this day.
Mighty impressive, wouldn't you say?
The birds love her berries, and I love their song.
When I look at her it just makes the day bounce along
like a buggy ride to town.

Well, you've seen what I've been doing over time.
You and I, though we're past our prime,
we can still split some kindling and wet a line.
We've trudged along, proving our worth,
sang a good song, sometimes in pain, other times in mirth,
with unseen help.

So let's go over the hill, here in back of my place.
I'll show you an old oak tree that has spirit and grace.
Four arms spanned can't measure her girth.
I know God planned for her to grace this spot of earth.
Do you see her from here on top of the hill?
We'll just go sit and lean against her until
she has told us what was and is, and how our cup to fill.
We can while away the hours unto the evening chill.

There was a time when my dad gave a pledge
while sitting against this tree, once surrounded by a hedge.
But since he's left this place so serene,
I've trimmed the hedge back, giving a view to the stream.
See there, weaving through the willows, like a dream.

I just thought of something—how long has it been
since you've been swimming bare bumpkin?
Quite a while, I'll bet. Come on, let's get wet
in that cool clear brook in the valley.

You ain't said much, I've been jabbering since you've been here
about such things as I have done.
I know you have a touch for spinning a tale.
You can clutch a mind like a fine heady ale.
You can bring to life times past no matter how stale.

So tell me now about the furrows on your brow,
the time your hounds never came back from the hunt.
You searched the woods from back to front.
If they went howling too far for you to follow,
you'd just leave your sweater lying in the hollow
to come back in the morning and find them sleeping on your sweater
and see them waiting for you, with their tails happily wagging.
There was nothing better.

You told me a black bear or the coyotes caught them.
How they'd run and howl, just like you taught them.
They loved to run free and loose like you and me.
They sure enough died trying and chasing game up a tree.
They would howl so loud when they'd tree their quarry.
Kind of like some folks we know, of who we are wary.
Am I right?

What's that, a tear in your eye?
Do times gone by bring thoughts of sadness to mind?
Oh, I understand, they're from the memories of friendships we find
for two old friends who've gone over the hill,
while enjoying life's treasures still.

Willie

To get my mind off you, I spun this tale—maybe two. That's
what I do. You can decide for yourself, is it true?

The Canadian Express, with a chill that gave no rest,
    from the north came calling my name.
A bitter chill churned by the gnawing wind, it
    was the chevron of the winter solstice.
The frigid air was expected but the snow had
    neglected to bless us with its cover.
In want of snow the relucent ice revealed the full
    moon's likeness on the half frozen lake.
I rose from my slumber; to the window I did lumber,
    expecting to see who's urging me to wake.
Through a spot I rubbed clear of frost on the pane,
    I could peer out over the lake once again.
To my dismay the spear house I placed that day
    had boarded the Canadian Express.
In panic I thought my shack would be brought to its demise
    as it skated toward open water.
I was anxious and in haste, all my efforts went to waste,
when I positioned my spear house over the monster's hideout so deep.
You see, when I moved here in June, the locals sang a
    tune of the Ada Lake lunker called Willie.
Well, my spear house didn't freeze to the ice, you see
and the insistent breeze waltzed my shack from its station.
So, in my pajamas and robe, barefoot as a toad, I raced across fiery ice
to intercept my spear house dancing with the wind so nice.
I caught it just in time to save its decline into
    the icy depths of Willie's home,
but the wind was too strong; I couldn't prolong
    that trembling shack's location alone.
With unknown strength, I guided it at length, my spear house,
over the ice to the shore, safe for the moment, nestled at the point
of the narrows, until I return in the morning fully awake.
Now running barefoot over ice is really not nice; hot coals I'd rather tread.

With frostbitten toes, I retired again to repose
in my heavily blanketed bed.
As my head hit the pillow, like a wisp of a willow,
I heard my name called with a laugh.
So once more I did plod to the window—was it God calling me?
No, it was Willie—he saw my gaff.
As my eyes searched the ice, I sought my mind for
advice on just how to catch Big Willie.
I recall old Hemp's tale about his travail the first time he saw Big Willie.
I laughed, for in his fable he said he was unable
to attack Big Willie for his fright.
Frozen in fear, he couldn't throw his spear at
Willie; he'd never seen such a sight.
Big as a gator, eyes ten inches wide.
He just sat and watched as Willie glided by his side.
Five years hence he saw him, still as tense in awe of him.
Said no man will ever set a jaw on him, Willie's
just too big, too fast, too smart.
Be careful if you go in skinny dipping, he could
bite your leg or tear you apart.
Now with all this behind me, I'll try to find
someone who'll listen to my tale
of a big fish called Willie who'll make you feel
silly, maybe even stupid and frail.
Big as a gator, his eyes will strike terror in hearts
and minds of any invader of his trail.
Now, the very next morning, I retrieved my spear house and replaced it
just exactly where old Hemp first saw Big Willie.
The ice was still scary thin—if it should crack, I'd have to swim
back to shore, to save my foolish soul.
I put aside my apprehension, and I want to mention,
the ice was only one inch thick where I cut the hole.
Instead of two feet square, I cut it three feet square
to be sure it would be big enough for Willie and me.
Determined, if I had to, I'd even be glad to go in after Willie if need be.
So, I gave it two or three days just sitting there empty on the ice.
Let Willie get used to seeing my vice.
He could see it above him from his thirty-foot-deep lair
because the water was clear and clean as the air.
On the edge of the drop–off, eighteen-feet-deep, the weeds stop growing.

The ledge was steep, and the bottom fell off to thirty feet.
I could watch Willie through this icy hole patrol his domain like a king.
If I were motionless and quiet as a cadaver so stiff, I might see Willie,
that is if he wants to be seen.
Now if you've never been in a spear house spearing fish left and right,
even Eskimos will tell you stories of their fright,
and of the one that got away by cunning, size, or might.
I'm telling you, the dreams will awaken you at night.
Big Willie likes sucker minnows big as shoe.
If you should fall in, he might eat you.
Arms stretched wide couldn't measure him from his nose to his dorsal fin.
I'd lower that sucker minnow in a harness to about twenty feet deep.
Big Willie would rise from the bottom to see what's to eat.
Before I could get him to rise any higher, he'd tear up my tackle,
eat my bait minnow, smile, and retire.
For about a month, we played cat and mouse,
Willie in his lair, cold, bright and green,
while I'm in my shack warm and dark and serene.
Well, this one day I raised my bait to about five feet deep,
because I could feel myself nodding off to sleep.
My bait would stay alive and be safe at that depth.
Maybe Willie's gone up to the bay for some bass, I guess he's left,
when from my dozing, my eyes started seeing
a log or a deadhead approaching my being
just beneath the ice, just a few feet below me.
With an intimidating smile, Big Willie just lay
there looking at me while I was sleeping.
I have to tell you I awoke with a start. Big Willie
was stalking me—oh, my heart!
He saw my eyes open wide made a one-eighty so fast,
I know he was hoping, here's a meal that will last.
I didn't go near that spear house until spring,
before the rains would bring a welcome thaw to take it off the ice.
When I put a for sale sign on my spear house that summer,
all the locals could say is, "What a bummer.
Now who's going to be the next fool to try and get Ole Willie?"

A true tale, spun by your pal.

This Child

This child, Lord, how pleasing you have made her!
This child, Lord, has pleased her mother dear.
This child, Lord, please keep her growing stronger,
and always, Lord, keep her heart to you near.
Oh, breathe your breath of life upon her.
Oh, keep her, keep her always in your hand
and let the light of your love shine within her
and forever guide her to help her stand.
Let her be your heart, your heart's desire.
Let her always be by your side
and always, always, Lord, take her higher,
and let her in your loving grace always abide,
for you've blessed us again with your comfort,
and you've continued always with your grace.
Strengthen her for all the days before her,
through understanding eyes and a smiling face,
for this child, Lord, how we thank you for her.
This child, Lord, has pleased those who are near.
Keep this child, Lord, growing ever stronger,
and these simple words of thanks I know you hear.

Dyanne

If the world could see through Dyanne's eyes,
there would be only sunshine and blue skies.
If the world had a heart like hers alone,
any place you are would be like home.
Only a soul so warm and kind
can know your thoughts and how to find
the inner you. You hardly know
the person you are but afraid to show,
until Dyanne looks into your soul.
If only the world were as generous as she,
its needs and hurts would never be.
If the world only knew how to feel as Dyanne,
we'd all be living closer to God's plan.
A gentle spirit like an angel's breath,
unveiling the bounty of a selfless death,
awakening in you a calming sense,
bringing down barriers of feeling tense,
when Dyanne talks with you.
As sure as God has given the sun and the rain,
He also has given us our sweet Dyanne,
for unto each other she blesses us all
warmth and refreshing as rain in the fall.
We thank you, God, for our sweet Dyanne.

Note: *This poem was purchased at a thrift store for fifteen cents. It was handwritten by an American prisoner of the Korean War. I have not been able to locate the author or his presumed sweetheart to whom it was written. Because of its emotional context of hopelessness, I was moved to express my feelings and honor this unknown hero for his pain and suffering. As a tribute to all the military personnel who have served, I was compelled to include his poem "Robin" in my book of poetry.*

Robin

Elusive winds of truth—
at times they drift so close
that pain and fear are overcome by
fevered expectation, the feeling that
a notion lost or gained will mean
the gain or loss of life itself.

And all the while I sense the ache
and loneliness behind a wall of tainted
minds, floundering in seas of painted
smiles.

A sea of boredom swallowing the isles
of hope and faith. The sense of lacking
that which justifies it all. But most of
all the fear of unacceptability. The force
that pulls our minds to roost on
murky shelves— opaque but never clear.

And still the loneliness persists. Our minds
and lives of time are sunken treasures of
a sea of dreams we never really come
to understand.

by Nate Halfrin

Pathos

A poignant rage within and unsettled thought.
Foregone conclusions pierced to naught.
A mind turned against itself,
struggling to dust off cobwebs of contradictions
from its shelf of disappointments and despair.
I sense a loss of faith in the intrinsic good.

I pray that if ever I should become so melancholy
as to relinquish my trust,
my God would lift me from such depths.
I must believe thus.
The words of a prisoner in a camp of doom,
like driven rain,
have touched my soul.
I felt his gloom. I felt his pain.
I have compassion and empathy
from such pathetic verse,
and like a knife his words so terse
cut my heart into bits and pieces.
How can a man write such a morbid thesis?

He felt total futility in a position of helpless need,
resigned to his fate, in perplexity by his captors' greed.
His faith is gone, no hope to grasp,
no charity tangible, the sting of an asp.

I am compelled to comment on Halfrin's poem.
He has divulged an inner Mephistophelean,
uncovering the cruelty of man.
However, I choose to trust in divinity,
the Creator's plan and the Trinity.
Yet I must accept the sinfulness of man.

One Angelic Kiss

One angelic kiss,
soft as a whisper
and given so tender,
to always remember,
clutched in a heart that won't forget
its deep beating when first it met,
that gossamer spirit.

Only an angel would ever a kiss share,
such a treasure from a spirit so rare
to lift a heart to heights above
previous thoughts of unrequited love.
Oh, that endearing spirit.

Sweet, sweet kindness,
sweet, sweet love.
When kissed by an angel,
kissed by an angel of love.

One angelic kiss freely given without a request,
Gentle and loving, giving rest,
to any doubts or fear in my breast.
To be kissed by an angel is
to be truly blessed.

My Dream

I was with an angel last night. Although only a dream,
it seemed so real.
The spirit of love and tenderness was within us.
Together we could feel away from the crowds of people,
in our world complete.
We were at a garden party with flowers and greenery,
divine in their fragrance—
primrose, magenta, all shades of pink, aqua, and blue
of a certain soft hue.
The pathway we walked led to a gazebo
made for two.
Across from each other, together we held hands
as our spirits soared.

As the eagle soars toward heaven,
as the hummingbird hovers before a flower,
as the ocean caresses the seashore,
as the mountain rises from the plain,
as the sunflower turns toward the sunshine,
as the lily opens to the rain.

I know I was with an angel, and I know I'll see her again.
She certainly was an angel—although only a dream, she was real,
real as the fragrance around her.
Alive was my heart beside her, telling me to bow low.
I kissed her feet—like alabaster they did glow.
She said rise to me and you will see,
I am your special angel heaven has sent to thee.
So encouraged by her loveliness I rose
to heights unknown before.
As the clouds reached for the stars,
as the moon follows Venus and Mars,
I know I saw an angel. I know I will see her again.
When will my angel return to me?
In my reverie, until then,
my dream remains with me.

The Thought of Your Kiss

Good morning, love, I come to you as a dove
on outstretched wings a-fluttering.
I'm trying to say in my peculiar way
what is in my heart without stuttering.

I tremble like this with the thought of your kiss.
I'm weak with excitement, can you tell?
If you come to my side, love will abide.
I am under your spell.

I'm enchanted like this from a single kiss
which you gave me without hesitation.
Since that day and every following day,
I dream my dream in anticipation.

If I could be your knight on a white horse,
I'd be gallant and brave—and shiny, of course.
You would ride in your gilded surrey.
All banners would wave in a colorful flurry
and my dream would be a reality.

Awakening

In the slowly lifting haze of morning twilight,
I watch from my secluded balcony
through tree branches swooning from the soft
kiss of a chilling spring breeze.
As I gaze past fluttering leaves stubbornly clinging to their mother tree,
I see the rooftops glistening with dew and the
distant hillside across the valley.
I notice the curling smoke rise from the chimney
tops, wafting upward in the mist.
The morning's vapor silently calls to my inward urgings
in a voice subtle and sweet as a mother's lullaby.
It is enticing my wandering spirit into a discourse with my heart,
toward thoughts and feelings previously recognized
but deferred till now for acceptance.
As I delve into the depths of my reticent heart's impressions,
I'm attempting to draw them out of a wellspring
of long past experiences and aspirations,
expecting that I will come to the crossroad's of my heart's wanting.
From whence comes forth my panting to flee from this cage
of unfamiliar, unexplained pensiveness?
I become aware of this singular reed in my heart awakening,
a sprouting of inferences like seeds,
pressing upward, out through the expansive tundra of my memories.
I must wait for the low winter sun to rise high
above to scatter the restraining hoarfrost
when the inner latent urgings will again begin
to blossom like the edelweiss.
I am impatient for the return of summer.

I'm uneasy in my anxiousness, knowing but not
knowing, caring but not sharing.
In humor I quietly chide myself for my quandary.
A smile lifts from my heart as I watch the roosting mourning doves
perched gingerly on their high wire.
They do a balancing act in the breeze as they
turn in practiced ritual fashion.
First they face west, where they said good night to the setting sun.
Then they face the east and welcome the anticipated sun to their new day.
Suddenly and seemingly with great purpose, they lift themselves in unison,
rising skyward in revelry,
convolving in their game of chase and be chased
as they stretch their sleepy wings in serious rolls and sudden dives.
Like children jubilantly playing with an imaginary
airplane in a display of flying acrobatics.
Amused, I return to my thoughts once more and
wonder how the caged bird can sing,
Or the Percheron be so nimble, or the indentured laugh,
or the eunuch be faithful, or the hunted sleep
knowing the stealthy hunter will never rest.
The blind go forth probing with a stick in faith. The
deaf find their delight in color and form.
While the halt may evoke a poignant twinge of compassion,
their determined optimism is infectious.
So why might I feel downtrodden?
Though the curtain is parted, the veil remains.
Only vaguely do I see beyond that which was hidden from my senses.
I am left with only conjectured theory contrary to my discipline.
If I attempt to reason the unreasonable, is it folly?
Whence does understanding come?

Does tolerance and patience ameliorate a breach?
Why is revenge so bitter? Should a brigand restore seven fold?
Life itself is a conspicuous stockade in which
the prisoner can only wait and watch,
without a jailor to provoke
while the apathetic transitory onlookers pass by
like dolphins racing against the waves.
The wolf howls in the moonlight from his den high upon a distant hill
with a forlorn lonesome call, his instincts to fulfill.
The partridge drums from atop a rotted stump;
his timeless urgings demand that he thump.
A noisy cricket hidden beneath some fallen leaves,
rubs his legs feverishly, his mate to please.
The mother giraffe kicks her newborn to rise to its feet.
Instinctively, it knows where to eat.
Salmon return from the ocean to spawn;
they are drawn back to the stream where they were born.
But man in his fervor to understand why is brought to humble tears.
Only man can cry.
Now the heart, we know, is at fault for this,
as the heart cries out for a lover's kiss.
For the heart has many a fault.
It must be recalled occasionally for renewal reasons
in order to become fully functional
or to be dependable to sustain through all seasons.

Why Hasten Tomorrow?

Hurry, tomorrow, hurry.
Can I hasten tomorrow?
There is a measure in a thing—
wait to see what tomorrow may bring.

I'm anxious, not for tomorrow,
but for what tomorrow may contain.
Happiness and joy to borrow,
no more strife or pain?

But what of pain?
For without pain,
would we recognize joy?
Or would it be another ploy?
To what abandon will I be receptive?
Why hasten tomorrow? It might be deceptive.

Could I?

How fleeting these short hours,
these times you spend with me,
sweet notions and sweet thoughts
when your sweet face I see.
The early summer grows, with lilies maturing,
the flowers bloom again so gay.
I'm enraptured by your smile alluring.
This summer will be mine always.
Your soft voice is calling me again and again,
echoing in my mind all day,
sweeter than the sweetest refrain.
Oh, how splendored the month of May,
lovelier than an etude in three quarter time.
Yet I yearn for so much more
than just these precious memories of mine
although I'm blessed more than ever before.

Can contentment come from just seeing you?
How can all my desires ever be fulfilled?
Your captivating smile, your eyes of blue,
I believe, to me these have been willed,
with beauty bestowed on a heart so pure,
a queen of queens, an enchanting dove.
I'm in the presence of an angel, I'm sure.
For to me, all I see is love.
Sweet angel, if indeed you're mine,
and you are my beloved song,
why do I languish for the time,
the time I'll know we belong?
Oh, those fleeting hours we're together,
they hurry by,
so quickly, quickly they are spent.
Could I enclose them within till you are nigh?
Through summer and winter, till all time is spent.

I Saw an Angel

I saw an angel's smile, I heard an angel's sighs.
I felt an angel's breath.
I looked into an angel's eyes.
I know she was an angel,
for an angel's breath is sweet.
She made my world much brighter.
An angel I did meet.

Oh, to see again that angel's smile
and to hear again her soft sighs!
To feel once more her very breath,
and search further the depth
of her blue eyes!
Not just once was I aware
she was an angel standing there
smiling at me as if to say,
come with me, come this way.

As often as I would see her,
as often she would smile.
Quickly I became accustomed,
to her presence all the while.
I knew not how to greet her,
for I was unable to speak.
Frozen in awe and wonder,
my very bones turned week.

She knew my every weakness,
she knew my every strength.
She came to me in meekness
and stilled my fears at length

As a soft breeze passes on by,
as a rainbow goes forth in the sky,
as rustling leaves on a wooded trail,
as the cool brook wanders through yonder vale,
each reminds me that she was here.
Though she is not beside me,
I can feel her ever near.

I long to look into the depth of her eyes,
to hear again her soft and tender sighs,
to feel once more her every breath,
to see again her captivating smile.
I yearn to be with her again,
if only for a while.

Where Is My Heart?

Where is my heart?
Since we met it is lost,
lost to a utopian dream,
lost in love's stream.

Love overflowing, not contained,
lost in love unrestrained,
lost forever in your grasp,
lost to my last dying gasp

I search for it without rest.
You have seized it from my breast.
All that I was has left,
for my heart has been cleft.

I live only because of you.
I dwell on the very thought of you.
My day is empty through and through.
My heart has been stolen—what do I do?

If comes a time when
you give it back again,
my heart will know then.
It will never be the same.

What to do?

I love you!

You have led me to paradise.
From the first look into your blue eyes,
my heart beat and breath did rise.
I realized you had seized my heart.

It is better in your clutches.

Imprisoned in Love

You've captured my heart,
carried it away.
You'll always have it with you
forever.
Through all time
till the world stops it's turning,
no longer is it mine.
It's yours to keep,
to keep
within your deepest treasures,
for you to possess completely
because you cherish it.
It's all I can give
but it's filled with my love.

You've taken my heart
and all that I am, dear.
And I know that you will
that you will take good care of it.
I'm empty now,
so in love with you,
for all that I was
is now at your command.
You see I cannot stand
without you now.
I'm your prisoner in love.

Lovely Is the Night

Lovely is the night when I am with you.
Lonely is the night without you.
I miss your blue eyes smiling at me,
though I can close my eyes and see them.
I long to taste your sweet lips and then
inhale your sighs as you breathe them.
My thoughts of you bring to me again,
the pleasant memories of our closeness when
we are together.
Although we are apart,
I can feel our togetherness
because I have given to you my heart.

Gusto

The kettle is simmering—don't lift the lid.
Savor the aroma—it won't for long be hid.
My mind is as a kettle of delectable stew.
My thoughts are like spices
for the broth which is you.
Meat and taters, carrots and maters, an onion too.
Don't raise the heat, it won't make it tender.
Let it simmer and suffer its flavor to render.
With the fire low all the fixin's combine.
Anticipation of its piquancy is realized in time.

Companionship

What comfort there is now—I can see another ship just off my bow.
Weeks alone on waves uncaring,
what solace, another sharing the high seas.

With spanker sail calling to follow her wake,
her flying jib billowing with all the wind she'll take,
main sails set with rigging to so taut,
a smart lady she is, this ship that has wrought
her fellowship here on the high seas.
Shall I come alongside her or just follow in her wake?
Surely she's the captain's pride.
She flaunts her sails and her teak wood strake.

The wind is favorable, the sunset is red.
The straits are only a few days ahead.
With good sailing and summer nights short,
we'll soon be anchored in an alluring port.

Though from a different harbor in a distant nation,
we'll come together in our common destination.
She's like an enchantress dancing
with silken gowns flowing.
Our companion ship has my heart glowing
here on the briny.

Musings of a Candle Lover

To pen a poem about a candle
is not an easy task to do.
To find proper words I can handle,
I'll simply relate a candle to you.
Now to begin, I'll peruse a candle's function.
Is spiritual soothing its destined unction?
I say nay. Nay, I say yea.
Is a candle to spread light round about?
To make the darkness flee? No doubt!
Hence, to shed light on the before unseen,
stirring the heart, the mind, the soul serene.
Another thought is of the warmth it gives.
When set in a window, I know someone lives,
and loves, I say, and loves.
But wait—my pondering recalls the essence
of a candle's ability.
Its aroma enhances the light with its fragrance,
arousing dreams from tranquility.
Lingering, lingering through the night
with a sweet perfume.
My worries and cares take flight
while shadows dance to the flickering light
across the room.

A candle's flame dancing encourages my imagination,
reaching the depth of my hearts palpitations
with feelings of love in all its variations.
Ah, to think a candles flame could instill
the common man to search his will,
and determine his vision to fulfill.
How is a candle like unto thee?
Just light a candle and you will see.
Behold, the feelings of serenity.
Repose, as dreams unfold to thee.
I'm drawn to a candle's undulating flame,
its warmth and its light doth proclaim
a comforting in the chill of the night.
A fragrance of oils from the tongue of fire
heightens my awareness, rouses my desire.
I come alive by a flame such as yours.
Your glow reaches every corner of my heart
while your fragrance will not part.
Dare I approach the flame eternal?
Will heaven reproach my impetuosity infernal?
Peradventure, should my heart be seared,
if I explore the warmth, the light, the fragrance revered?
Will I ever know? How will I know
if the candle's glow and fragrance should flow
over my heart? Will it abide if I were to begin
to gratify this hiatus?

In Her Kitchen

Angel's in her kitchen,
a little corner of heaven.
I know I'll like what she's fixin',
and she doesn't need any leaven'.

Honey roasted hot cross buns
and vul-au-vent supreme,
a glass of Darjarnea
with a little Menthe de Crème.

I watch her move so effortlessly
as on Mercury's feet she floats.
Her fingers are like a dancer's to me,
with their pirouetting strokes.

I am fascinated by her rhythm
and her inimitable grace.
I'm celestially bound right here
in heaven's kitchen space.

All my days I've wondered
about feminine pulchritude.
My days are no longer numbered—
I've found beauty in magnitude.

Overflowing constantly,
like a beaver dam in spring,
there just is no containment
for such a beautiful thing,
as an angel
in her kitchen.

Feeling Like Reeling

If at times I'm overbearing,
too much conversation I must be sharing.
Forgive me.
I'm intoxicated.
If at times you find me boring and
you catch me almost snoring,
forgive me.
I'm inebriated.
If when my speech is somewhat meaningless
and you're disinterested,
nonetheless I guess
you'll forgive me.
I'm under the influence, you see.
I know when conversation starts to slow.
I lose my charm—my thoughts,
they're wont to flow.
I'm dizzy.
Forgive me.
I feel as though I'm left holding the bag
when our banter begins to lag
because I'm in a stupor.
Forgive me.
It's your entire fault, you see,
because you're super.
Your intoxicating kiss,
your inebriating bliss, has such an influence on me.
An imbiber lost in a wisp of a wish,
forgive me.
I'm dizzy, reeling, and kneeling.
Forgive me.
This old bloke longs to soak
in your love.

If

If I were to descend to the depths of the sea,
what form of treasure would I find there to be?
If I were to climb to mountain heights above,
what would be there for me to love?
If as an eagle I could soar through the air,
would I find fulfillment there?
If the desert should bloom for me alone,
would that be the greatest joy to have known?
If the birds of the forest sang my lullaby,
would tears of happiness overflow my eye?
And what treasure is found in caverns so deep,
visions of grandeur when I close my eyes as in sleep?
If my rose garden bloomed all year long,
would that be more gratifying than a meadow lark's song?
I try to recall my most exhilarating time—
to what great heights did my beating heart climb?
Did I relish the sun on my forehead all day
or the rain on my back and shoulders as it lay.?
Or the frostbitten cheeks and my lips that would crack,
or that nagging pain and stiffness in my back,
or that stubborn knee that doesn't bend
when the growing season decides to end.?
What of the scent of the earth just turned by the plow?
Can I tell you more of my enchantments just now?
A wild blueberry picked when just right?
What is my favorite delight?
The campfire crackling with its lonesome smoke
that wants to be near you and makes you choke
and sparks like fireflies rise above
while sharing tales of the past, future, things you love.
There are so many good things in life such as this.
But the best of all is your tender kiss.

Let This Heart

Your winsome eyes, your lilting laughter,
your wistful smile is before me through all time.
Your warm and tender heart will remain with me ever after,
for with your presence I have become entwined.
I don't understand this unfamiliar rapture
or why I am immersed in dreams divine.
I must survive this inner fiery chapter,
this consuming longing and urging of mine.
Just let these feelings travel higher.
Let this beating heart be worthy.
You know so well how I aspire
to abandon all things earthly.
Just let these hands caress you always.
Just let these arms enfold you round about.
Just let these eyes drink endlessly of your beauty.
For all your loveliness my soul cries out.
Every day seems to pass too slowly
if I don't hear your voice or see your face.
Someday, when all things will be holy,
I will fully know your boundless grace.
Just let these hands feel good with what they're holding.
Just let this heart beat in rhythm to yours.
Just let this mind never ponder things unfolding,
for the warmth and love of one has many doors.
Every day without you is disturbing.
I just can't get to the reason of it all.
I find my answers don't come easy
and maybe even there is no answer at all.
Just let these arms hold you forever.
Just let these hands never let you go.
Just let this heart forget you never
and learn of you all I want to know.

This Little House

This little house on top of the hill,
I am hopeful now, will time stand still?
This little house has been filled with love.
It is nestled there with trees above
and so appealing just to see it there
with flowers all around, they are so fair.
The sound of laughter, birds singing their melodies,
even the breeze does sing as it caresses the trees
ever so gently.
Oh, I love to see that little house
nestled there upon the hill.
It lingers on my mind, and I am
yearning to return.
Return to this little house I know I will.
I have memories that return again and again,
the precious memories of joyous times when
all the world was bright and open fields were in sight.
When I look at the moon each night
the soft glow of the evening's starry light
brings back memories of that night in June.
Oh, that first night that I held you tight,
and everything was just so right.

As I looked into your eyes so blue and bright,
I saw such love as I've never seen before.
And darling, so much more.
My heart was beating so, your very being did glow,
and the world was waiting to know
if I would show you the love
for which you have always yearned.
Would-be lovers you have spurned,
even though their hearts were burned
by your love and beauty.
You saved this love for someone,
for someone who would love you
the way in which you would want them to.
In your heart you knew you did right.
That night you shared with me alone.
No one else has known
the silent wings of ecstasy.
This came upon the two of us alone
in the rapture of one another.
There is no other bliss ever quite like this.
Woven together by a kiss,
let us cleave to each other,
just as this little house has become
part of the hill, nestled in the trees,
just as we are one.

My Redd

Like foaming waves
my sea of emotions keeps rolling in,
comes rolling in always,
never ceasing, always increasing,
as the tide.
Be it neap or be it high,
it fills my soul so deep,
it thrills my soul to keep,
it disturbs my soul from sleep.
These foamy waves of my musings,
they caress my feelings,
bringing completeness to my being.
Whether the setting sun,
the full moon, clouds or misty dew,
they kiss my thoughts,
with an ovation of the joy of being.
Don't tell me, I know I'm a dreamer,
a lover of the changing seasons,
an observer of life and reasons.
I watch and am glad for them all,
for each new wave of urgings renewed,
of thoughts subdued,
a progression toward the horizon of awareness,
the intrigue of adventure into remote thoughts.
Though what is afar I'm sure I am called to nurture,
the unrelenting foamy waves of interpretation and recognition,
as I am enthralled by the passing waves over my anchorage.
My harbor, my solace, as I regress into the mooring place of my dreams,
My introspection of success and rejection,
in recollection, fondling each thought as though it were a grain of sand
on the shifting shoreline of my retreat.

In My Persuasion

Truth, I am in want for truth.
A believer.
Even when in want, I'm a believer
in truth.
In truth, is the heart a deceiver?
They say it is.
But in truth, what best to reason with
in self-exploration but the heart?
A search in need to realize verity.
Search my heart.
An endeavor accepted, unopposed
by truth, a rarity.
Search in truth my heart
until the vague is obvious
and the obvious vague.
So I ask myself within myself,
Heart, what is true?
Tell me in total, not in part.
Is this internal wresting virtuous?
At times I would challenge, it is spurious,
but in truth I am constrained by my task to ask.
Is this my persuasion?
Does my search for truth
bring me closer to what I am in want of?
Tell me, Heart.
My intrinsic nature is enhanced by this desire.
This love at rest,
with my natural being, my soul my spirit.
For truth as its quest.
I must confront that which I cannot see
or hear with my heart.
Oh, tell me, Heart, today, must I remain in yesterday?
Must I go on in want this way?
Must doubts and fears always stay in my heart?
Will they part if I follow my heart?

On the Sea of Love

It was the fourteenth of June, just another
afternoon gig at the Friday happy hour.
I was playing my music for the old timers and
sitting alongside a pretty flower.
We played every song that came to mind and even some they didn't know.
That pretty flower next to me played so brilliantly the room started to glow.
I thought I heard the angels singing every song in harmony so sweet
While everyone clapped hands in time and tapped out with their feet.
Then I looked at the flower beside me; she
winked and smiled her special smile.
We played and played while the dancers swayed
and champagne bubbled awhile.
Now a day like this comes but once in a blue moon,
and I knew it was all going to end too soon.
We kept on playing our music anyhow.
It was like heaven, I remember even now.
I know that pretty little flower enjoyed it too,
by her smile and azure eyes so blue
that told me everything I didn't know, and more.
I'd never felt so complete at any time before.

Let me tell you now, the ending was better than the beginning—
you can believe it.
If another time comes by like that again, I'll retrieve it.
We played the last song that day in June just for our own pleasure
with a fascinating rhythm in close harmony,
and variations in time and measure.
The music we made for each other that day, the whole world is longing for.
We played, and we stayed in close harmony
and repeated each refrain once more.
And the angels were singing and the chimes were ringing
in a symphony of unashamed love.
Even the stars in the sky came low from above
like moths to a burning flame.
Words cannot describe the tenderness of our song,
gentle as the rising tide, carrying us along.
Higher, ever higher our spirits lifted with the flow.
How well we were aware of that irresistible undertow,
as the foamy waters nudged us ever further into the bay.
We clung together hoping to stay that way.
As we abandoned our efforts to resist the tide,
we drifted into obscurity in the hazy mist to abide,
to abide in the sea of love.
Words cannot describe the tenderness of our song

My Song

Pretty bluebird, I'm as lonesome as I can be.
Little bluebird, sing your song again for me,
your song so dear every morn, your song of cheer.
I forget I'm forlorn when your song I hear.
There was a time I had a song like you.
Will you sing for me? I'm so blue.
Do you sing for another now, every day?
Come sing your song to me, come this way.
I'll watch and listen as my achy heart you still.
Will you come to my window with your bright trill?
I seek you in the meadow and listen for your song.
I hope to see you there through the day so long.
Is that you I see on yonder garden rail?
Perhaps you'll be singing in the shady grassy vale.
I'll wander to the brook with hope to find you there.
Your song will ease my mind of all my worldly care.
I long for your dear melody once more,
for the return to the memories of our times before.
My heart will be much lighter then,
though I know not where, I know not when.
So I'll keep in my heart your lovely refrain.
Your memory is sown deep—it will remain.
I'll water and nurture it as a perfect rare flower
and hope someday it will grace your ivory tower.

New Wine

You have poured new wine into this vessel worn over time
and filled me completely with the ether of your smile sublime.
With its ambrosia flowing I'm suddenly knowing the meaning of euphoria.
No longer am I empty—how will I contain this new wine?
They say it is foolish to reuse an old wine skin like me.
To hold you, even enfold you, I am willing.
Though I should burst, it would be my fulfilling.
So I'm anxious to see how long I can hold thee.
I'll wait on your need and accept that which will be.
Can I endure your wine overfilling?
So pour your wine into this old skin made for one's thirst.
Let me savor the effervescence as the tiny bubbles burst.
You have instilled in my flask all that I ask and more.
Don't be concerned that this vessel was spurned before.
So pour freely, your wine unto me to the fill,
your wine distilled from the grapes of your hill.
You have seasoned it with an angel's sprinkle of dew,
wine incomparable as only could be made by you.
You've poured your new wine into this vessel of mine
in spite of its obvious wear over time.
I'm captured by the aroma of your wine—its bouquet fills the air.
I know I'll be thirsting for more. I'm parched from my wandering.
That I shall burst, you need not be pondering.
Fill my flask is all I ask, let your new wine be mine.

A Delicate Shade of You

A crescent moon lowering over the mountain top,
the night air gathering its dew to drop,
the descending moon tipping in the western sky.
The evening star Venus lingers affectionately nearby
seeming to beckon her companion to follow,
at other times lagging behind as if to allow
the changeable moon her own wanderings.
Wisps of clouds unsure of their patterning
drift sleepily in the lunar light flattering.
This night with soft moon light is nocturnal delight.

The nightingale is quiet now.
His serenade is through.
But if I wait and watch, somehow,
soon will perfect the foggy morning dew.
In the quiet of the filmy morning chill,
I hear a distant whippoorwill.
I wonder if he knows it's past three,
that the valley is sleeping,
but for him or me.

Now if I should answer his lonesome song,
would he fly to my side and stay until dawn?
These sleepless nights I deem precious,
brought forth by an emergence of thoughts so restless.
I have learned to regale these tranquil nights
and juggle my thoughts of esoteric delights
as when you come to me softly like the morning dew,
then envelope me completely with your scintillating hue.
To my delight, I find a delicate shade of you.

An Angel's Tear

Who am I that ever I should see an angel cry
when I thought tears were only for the weak?
So now I know I'd rather die
than to see tears falling on an angel's cheek.
I am so humbled by her love for another
who is bound by an unseen chain.
I have stumbled upon the love of a mother
and discovered the depth of her pain.
If it were in my power, this very hour,
I would take as my own her fear.
Like petals of a flower,
each tear should empower,
as a crown for a heart so dear.
Celestine eyes and golden hair, piety in her so demure,
I know now an angel does cry.
Her tears are like diamonds so pure.
Oh, how helpless I feel, in spite of my zeal,
for only faith will conquer her fear.

When my days seem harrowing and my path is narrowing,
and I call upon an angel's presence,
I know not in part but fully in my heart
how an angel's love is her essence.
As well, I have learned to love her, love is returned,
sevenfold times seventy.

With a heart that is burned
by a longing spurned,
an aura of grandeur heavenly,
An angel's tears can endure though the years,
in spite of toil and tribulation,
with a heart that is strong, able to prolong
the knowing and caring for her daughter dear.

My Heart's Song

This song in my heart comes to me freely
in unison with its beating,
my heart song of freedom,
in harmony with the melody repeating,
a freedom song lifting in legato,
flowing in the tones of tenderness,
a heart song of passion resolved in its tempo,
ebbing between measures with rests,
recurring rhythm, transitions in time.
I am overcome with their eloquence sublime.
It brings forth longing in every strain,
bubbling up a wellspring of desires which remain
endlessly flowing into dissonance, yearning for a resolution.
How long will this symphony sustain?
How long will I be able to contain
this lilting refrain
that has permeated my brain?
I cannot restrain that which is presented.
All stops must be pulled, my heart's timbre vented.
I would be content to drift off meter
knowing the theme is sweeter.
When a heart is tender
with a rendition of love to remember
in measure, in rhythm, in time,
my heart's song,
a song of freedom now I embrace.
I didn't lose my heart to a song,
the song came into my heart's space.

Don't Ask

If you could look into the depth of my soul,
you would find an endlessly drifting scroll
of phrases that rhyme, harmony sublime,
with dissonance that demands resolution,
soft tones, meter of sounds, sweeter than
those played or sung by man's convolutions.
This ecstasy of mine is like a calling divine.
It overwhelms any external intrusions.
To me it's a blessing,
to others it's just messing and
oft times creating allusions.
Some write with pen,
erase and write again.
Others build towers in the sky.
I write with my heart.
It's an urgent part
of me, I don't know why.

A Heart Embraced

The dew is heavy this September night.
The moon unseen, stars nowhere in sight.
A shiver from the chill of the brisk night air—
where you are, I wish I were there.
The fragrance of your hair,
your warming touch,
a night without you,
I miss you so much.
Dreaming of you, yearning for you,
these feelings I know oh so well.
Every beat of my heart, every breath does tell
of cloistered dreams that in my mind do knell.
I picture you in my mind,
I hear your voice so kind.
I think of your touch—
oh, how it means so much.
I feel the midnight dew on my shoulder.
if only I were bolder,
to say all that is within me.
So with pen I embrace your heart.
I'm able to say I yearn for you.
You have sprung open the gate of my heart
and started it beating again.

When You Are Near

Gliding to and fro on the front porch swing
with the clouds rolling by and the sun setting,
my arm over the shoulder of my loved one dear,
I sought heaven, and I've found it here.
A cool breeze blowing fallen leaves about,
my inner spirit ascending wants to shout,
but not to disturb this quiet moment of bliss.
I'll just lean closer to her lips for a kiss.
I shall never be able to speak
what my heart seeks to say
nor pen the words to describe this day.
I feel my heart anxiously beating true.
It's always this way when I'm near you.
The evening chill obliges a closer hug and squeeze,
perchance to hold her tighter—should I ask her please?
Oh, heart! She heard your plight and snuggled up,
closer. Everything's all right
this night.

Ecstasy

You fill me with ecstasy.
Darling, do you know
how you make my heart glow?
Fantasy?
It is not a fantasy!
My heart is beating fast,
from this spell you've cast.
What will it be?
You've made a new world for me
so I want to show
how my love flows.
Do you see
my love that flows so free?
Although I know our lives are so
differently woven with memories
from times past
and loves that last hauntingly,
your misty eyes consume me.
Your soft sighs echo in my mind,
endlessly.
I am reminded constantly
how dear you are to me
in my ecstasy.

Now I Lay Me Down to Sleep

Now I lay me down to seek
your special favors and kiss your cheek.
If I may lay close to you,
I will do all that you want me to.
I will tenderly enfold you in my arms
as I explore all your exotic charms,
caressing from toes to fingertips,
tasting and savoring your bewitching lips.

Shall I write more of what I will do,
or speak of love, my love for you?
My heart is filled with feelings sent
from heaven's gate to be spent,
spent in congruent desires and fascination
with softly repeated sighs of adoration.

So Rises My Heart

As though on wings,
my heart lifts to lofty heights unknown.
As though with strings,
it resounds in riffs of engaging tones.
Where once a tacit heart lay sleeping,
there is now a crescendo in its beating.
Toward heaven's golden gate it is fleeing,
carried on an angels wings
toward its destined celestial abode
where infinite delight in every mode
is exalted without measure.
An arabesque flight in rhapsody,
a jubilant strain of pleasure,
so rises my heart toward heaven's gate,
carried on an angels wings,
this heart once sedate.

Who Goes There?

Qui va la?

I am a traveler in time, a voyager in space,
a sojourner for now on this earth's face.
I am circling the sun while the moon circles me.
Now I have a new journey, unplanned.
I have no itinerary.
I am embarked on discovery,
eager to see what will be.
Though my life, my plans, and schemes
were filled with visions and dreams
of places and faces,
I began seeking traces of pathways in the sky.
I have sought a trail on the foamy sea
and scoured the horizon for what is to be.
With compass and chart and glass I searched
for a suitable stone on which this vagrant could perch.
I have scanned the mountain ranges from afar,
while flurries of snow caressed their peaks,
Once traversed the desert by light of star,
with windblown sand peppering my cheeks.
I dove for pearls in a tropical lagoon,
tepid and serene,
watched antelope graze by light of moon,
with aught between them and me.
I am a traveler in time.
Alive.
I live with this new inspiration of mine, a new star to follow.
Where it leads I allow.
all my senses titillated,
all my reason cultivated,
all my aspirations emancipated,
all my emotions elevated
by a new angel star.
For this star I have been questing.

To Capture Rapture

I would fain write a symphony
to proclaim your loveliness,
a sweet rhapsody filled
with words of tenderness.
It would be played by heaven's angel, Jubal,
on his alated harp of gold.
But alas, only an angel
could conjure words so bold
to describe your beauty wondrous
and your heart's ardent nature told.
Through the ages lovers and poets
have written pages of endearments
and bliss divine.
Now this childish heart dreams
of phrases and praises
that are solely mine.
It is my way to immortalize
every precious charm of you
each time unto time and time.

Daydreams

You're the one for whom I am yearning.
My longing grows as day to night is turning,
and always I find when day recedes
for your tender touch my heart pleads.
I am reminded of your touch
by a gentle summer breeze.
I hear your laughter
in a bird's song from the trees.
I think of a cool, clear, bubbly stream
and my heart wants to follow its dream.
But better my heart and soul are blessed
when we're together and together caressed.
In my eyes your beauty is most revealing.
Now in my heart, your kisses I am stealing.
I seek your warmth for all its comfort.
I seek your grace and all its comport.

I see white billowing clouds on high.
Are you dancing among them
like an angel in the sky?
Were I to see you with wings and psaltery
or golden halo,
it would not surprise me.
Would that I could see your face so loving.
This bleating heart would stop its roving.
I must allay this solitude of mine,
if just to look into your eyes divine,
so in this deep hope I am depending
on your enchantment never ending.

Since You Came Along

I have dreams of sunny meadows
and flowers all around,
a laughing stream where I have found
the welcome shade of a stately oak tree
where a bluebird calls to me
with a sweet refrain,
a melody of love
in harmony with my heart.
Since you came along,
I am enticed to rest
beneath its spreading branches.
With this beautiful tree, now my heart dances.
In my wanderings I have searched and did roam
for just such a tree in which to perch
a home
where peace and comfort abide with beauty.
I have known so long it's God's given duty
for each of us to find serenity like this,
for each to share one another's bliss.
My dream returns to me each night.
Now I wake each morning with vibrant delight
since I have found in my dream a reality.
How wonderful the world is when you're with me.
Since you came along.
in the cool morning mist,
the layered mountains are kissed
by the sun yet low,
caressing with its glow
my heart.
My heart sings its song
as morning brings
these wonders to my world.
Now I know the rapture
since you came along.

My House

In this little house of mine,
which has been forged over time,
I have found comfort to no end.
There is joy and peace in the time I spend
in this little house of mine.
From my windows I see beyond the mountains.
At my doorstep I drink from sparkling fountains.
Before my fireplace I see your face,
and in my den, there you are again.
In this little house I call mine,
I can hear your voice echoing in the hall,
A soft whisper like a sweet loving call.
I go to my garden;
you are there
with pretty little flowers all in your hair.
Lingering within this little house of mine.
Oh, to describe the feelings inside
since you've come to reside
in this little house of mine.
There are no walls, nor roof, nor beams.
Only these visions of grandeur, it seems,
since you've come to reside
in this little house of mine.
Am I too vague? I'll try to explain.
How you've blessed my house I do proclaim.
This humble hovel, this shelter mine
has become a palace gilded, divine.
No wind, nor rain, nor storm strong
will ever put asunder, no matter how long.
Nor will it overturn the golden chalice.
Of my fortress, my house, my very own palace.
And yet this little house of mine
is now for you for all time
with your love in this palace of mine.

My Hajji

You have thrown to me your lifeline of love.
To thank you, I'll gather the stars above.
The warmth of the sunshine is yours alone.
The radiance of the full moon mimics your tone.
Heaven's inspiration, of wonder designed,
is gathered together for the two of us to find.
How can I give you what is already yours?
The gate is unlocked, open are the doors.
All pathways now are bright with a hue
of fragrance and delight directly from you.
I'll never leave this state I'm in.
My wandering is finished.
Now in my repose I can begin
praise in prose and poetry of you.
This is my hajji, my destiny true.
This is my Mecca, my flight, your love to accrue.

For You Only

I kiss your forehead,
my face turns red.
I kiss your lips,
oh, how my heart skips.
I kiss your neck,
I'm a wreck.
Then I get bolder and kiss your shoulder,
then come to rest upon your breast.
Rapid beats my heart in increasing legions
as I depart toward further regions.
Your chest heaves with rapturing swells.
This exhilaration we've captured dwells.
Your urgent sighs incite me to continue.
As I kiss your thighs I begin to
explore your hips with my searching lips,
while caressing your toes with my fingertips.
Now is the time that we discover
the wonder, the ecstasy of a tender lover.
We're enveloped in one another's embrace.
This is our time, this is our space.
We sought paradise right here on earth.
We have found heaven is a reachable berth.

With You

When I lay with you
and I say to you
words you want to hear

a thousand years is like a day with you
while I stay with you
to spend in play with you,
near ever so near.

My ship is in the bay with you,
anchored, so to play with you.
Love will never fray with you.
Year after year after year.

My Anxious Heart

What an exquisite freshness I have found in you.
Your happiness emanates like sunshine in skies of blue,
an aura of mystique to behold,
crisp thoughts which lead to deep talks
of feelings before untold.
Intrinsically caring
Infinite love
Quiet and graceful,
like a dove
our spirit moves,
inspiring an empty heart to be filled.
For all this I see in my angel who has stilled
my anxious heart.
I have now a calmness we all desire.
There is in each of us an eternal fire.
Now I have a fullness for which I aspire.
What do I lack? What more need I acquire?
I search my innermost self for this thought
and only tranquility is wrought,
in a formerly anxious heart.

When We Are Apart

How tedious and tasteless these hours without you near.
I long to hear your voice and gaze into your blue eyes so dear.
The low winter sun has lost its warmth for me.
The chill in this lonesome darkness is oh so dreary,
but then I think of you and what to me you mean
and I find myself saying your name aloud
Sweet Barbara Jean. Oh, sweet Barbara Jean.
The flowers will bloom again when I hold you in my arms.
As like other times when I'm enveloped in your charms,
I speak your name out loud—to me its music so dear.
I imagine you in my mind and your essence is near.
Though winter is icy, my reverie of your song
brings summer to my heart and my desires prolong,
and I know so well how my heart beats swell
with every thought of you.
The caring in my heart for you will always dwell,
with each memory of every moment a spell.
I shan't be content with only a memory,
as sweet as memories are.
Albeit,
I am content knowing, soon I'll be where you are.
Although the seasons change,
colors of flowers rearrange.
All the while my heart contains
sweet refrains of our times together.
This is my song of happiness,
My prayer with your name on each breath,
my way to pass every hour of each day,
in my fancy of you.
When we are apart,
you're always in my heart.

If We Could Share

If we could share a time or two
as we go along our way,
I'd truly care about the time with you
each moment of the day.
It would still my bleating heart for you
in gladness for the time.
For each moment we're together is
only yours, only mine.
Happiness would bloom in our hearts again
like flowers in a meadow lane.
Life would be then complete.
It would never be the same.
Our dreamy thoughts of what could be,
our laughter and tears we'd share
with hearts in fullness of love replete,
in each moment that we care.
I'm offering now in manner meek
to share all my heart with you,
for true happiness is ours to seek.
It is life's force in all we do.
This world is kind to those who love
unceasingly, it is so.
Caring and sharing, giving and loving
is all a heart yearns to know.
For time and space in a common place
with a loved one there is a need
to put aside doubts or fears of love—
only then our hearts are freed.
I long to share all that I am
with an angel so true,
an angel in love's ageless plan.
That dear angel, darling, is you.

My Babe

My babe called early this morning.
I knew she was lonesome too.
I didn't have any loving last evening,
but I'm happy now just talking with you.
Now the sun is just arising,
bright and cheery on the horizon.
I'll just close my eyes and then
think of all the loving with you.
A sweet word to start the day
is so great, what can I say?
Only how glad to hear your voice,
although it's really my second choice
right next to being with you,
each time excitingly new.
So call me again and again,
early in the sleepy a.m.
I'm longing to see you soon.
Just as the stars with the moon
seek to show their splendor,
we'll be together again
to always remember.
My babe knows how to awaken me.

My Garden

I have a hidden garden,
a quiet retreat for thought
where in time with devotional pardon
a quiet heart is wrought.
The pathway to my quiet place
is a well-worn path I walk.
It is needful daily this path to trace
and with the garden spirit talk.
I have peace like a river flowing slow and sure,
and the spirit giver is bestowing love so pure.
I slowly walk with my bare feet on the earth
to better feel its sweet breath for all it's worth.
The earthy aroma carries my thoughts serene
like flowing streams toward rivers of peace,
rivers of dreams,
and
I am content.

A Noble Garden

Your love is like a garden, dear,
with flowers of every hue
in which my heart pants to be near
a cluster of your love so true,
our thoughts always like a deep mine
with diamonds rich and rare
hidden there for a time
for those who'd search with care.
Your eyes are like stars, a thousand rays of light.
They comfort this one who seeks a pathway in the night.
Oh, may I love your preciousness?
May I explore your hidden depths?
May I glean your fragrant flowers?
Oh, let your eyes as stars
guide this seeker's path.

Paradise Found

Silky soft shades of gray shadows lengthen.
Early evening dew drops like diamonds settle on velvet leaves.
Cool breezes subside, the wind chimes are still.
In quite reverence the song birds gather and watch
as the low winter sun descends behind the distant hill.
The venatic honeybees retreat to their trove,
eluding the twilight chill.
Day lilies in silent vespers are folding their petals,
Their delicate ivory flowers bowing and nettled.
I am overtaken with lofty thoughts and romanticisms.
My heart beats with a thrill.
Like garlands of colored whipped cream,
the clouds caress the mountain peaks at will
with a refracted display of the solar spectrum so bright
overlaying the shrouded forms below.
In the fading light a chill descends.
I hold dear the solemnity in which I reminisce our moments together.
Your charms are alive with every spark of euphoric thought
like fireflies illuminating in desire ever,
while my heart beats an echo to every cricket's trill.
My soul is anointed with your loveliness.
You have inspired me to bathe in the spring of Mount Parnassus,
and I know Apollo's profound joy
proffered by the sacred waters of Castalia.
I am immersed in explicatory rhyme in my nostalgia,
so deep in my heart is the ecstasy of our time
when we dare approach heaven together,
just the two of us soaring on high
soaring together forever

Time in Limbo

When we embrace, the universe is immobile,
held in place for a reason.
The planets and stars are motionless awhile,
static in space for a season.
They are suspended in time with our desire.
We are comforted by love's eternal fire.
All human forces are in equilibrium
while we tarry before heaven's propylaeum,
your lips pressing to mine,
our hearts beating in rhyme.
Still stands the time
as we entwine in love divine
at heaven's doorstep.
In our embrace our rapture is sustained
with rhythmic undulations, tenderness restrained.
Insistent whispers, urgent sighs
like sequential ocean waves as they rise
in muted sounds of ecstasy, caressing.
What greater love could there be
when so softly you come to me?
Each moment is an eternity
and the sun and the moon stand still,
extending time in limbo,
with love to fill our hearts in complete surrender,
forever to remember
as long as the sea abides the shore,
or until the world is no more.

From a Lily Pad

a frog's perspective

Would a graceful swan while floating by
notice a frog such as I?
Would she see the enchanted tear in my eye?
Would she stretch her wings for a moment?
I cry!
Beauty and grace such as I have never seen!
Her majestic feathers I feign would preen.
But what has a frog to do with a queen
who commands the very pond serene?
Would I be impertinent to seek her detection?
Would I be brazen to show my affection?
From my lily pad I gaze at her reflection,
too shy, to pavid to look in her direction.
Oh, heart be still!
She heard your beating.
Tis not my will
but I must be fleeting.
Heaven help me.
She has discovered my secreting,
she even smiled at me.
She's heard my bleating,
needeep, needeep, needeep.
Her neap I'll keep till I sleep in the deep,
as I have become very fond
of her exquisite presence in the pond.

My Song to You

Now I have a song to sing,
a song to comfort me through the night,
to soothe my aching heart,
to ease the sting of loneliness
and make everything all right.
Now my burden I can bear,
now my aspirations I can share.
With each repeated phrase,
I whisper a prayer of thankful praise.
Now I have a song to sing,
and like a child I shall sing with glee.
For now all seasons are as spring.
My song is of the love you bring
to me.

Your Azure Blue Eyes

I imagine your azure blue eyes,
Your whispers echoing tender sighs.
I am immersed in my reverie,
in dreaming of times you've been alone with me,
recalling times we have known,
all the love we have shown each other.
I can taste your inviting lips.
My anxious heart, oh, how it skips
with every thought of you—
these feelings and the love I feel
are oh so real.
I'll always remember, I shan't forget
the first time we met.
Your radiance filled the room
as an ester of azaleas in full bloom.
You were so discreet, with your smile so sweet.
I was caught in your captivating glance.
I didn't have a chance.
I was hopelessly enthralled in anticipation,
not knowing my fate in profound fascination.
Thus beats my heart again,
each time I reminisce
that time when
you gave me your first angelic kiss.

Why?

Why do I love you?
Not because I'm in heaven in your arms,
nor is the reason your many charms.
Not because I yearn for your touch
nor my excitement when in your clutch.
You, dear heart, I embrace
not for your beauty
nor for your grace,
but because you did bestow
your love toward me
so I would know
the warmth of love's eternal fire
to raise my awareness ever higher.
So ask not why the reasons,
accept my love for all seasons.
Shall I not love you purely?
You are my angel surely.
I cannot attain heaven's heights alone,
without your sweet leaven shown.
I draw deeply of your endowing breath.
It is like unto spring time reviving
flora from its winter sleep like death.
Your first glance
your first smile
your first kiss—
I am beguiled all the while in my bliss.
And so I love you and will eternally,
for the new heart you have given unto me.
Because you are love
and so, I can love.

Moment to Moment

For a moment my heart stopped
and I caught my breath
for it left
for a moment
when you first looked at me
for a moment.
You came near to me
and my heart beat feverishly.
I didn't know then
if you'd look my way again.
For a moment
I watched you
in a moment of wonder.
And then
all my senses went
asunder for a moment.
I thought an angel had caressed me
in that moment you looked my way.
Wonder of wonders,
that moment of wonder
when my heart stopped.

Your angelic breath
lifted my spirit from its depths.
Now my heart beats anew
because of you
in that moment.
My heart beats true from that moment,
now
each moment to moment
my heart pants for you,
waiting for your angelic touch
and for each moment
that I may empty my soul.
You have made me whole
in a moment.
You gave me so much
in that moment.
I was transformed
with one momentous kiss.
That is why I am like this,
not for a moment
but for all time.

To Italy with Love

My love has boarded the eastbound plane.
Till she gets back I won't be the same.
Already I can feel my poor heart crying.
She's hardly out of sight.
Oh, how I'm trying
to be strong, to be brave.
She knows that I will save
all my love for her return,
how I'd walk over hot coals
though my feet may burn.
Her love to me she did impart
to forever remain in my heart.
Although every day without her is tedious,
with her love she has given to me
I will not be frivolous.

Now my love is on to Atlanta by plane.
She is headed east, and I cannot refrain
from hearing my heart murmur over again,
the sweet assurance of her love enduring until then.

When her plane crosses the great sea
and arrives in Venice, the star of Italy,
my love will be so far from my arms,
yet I will be warmed by my memory of her charms.
I know she'll be as lonely as I in her travels,
but soon she'll return to tell me of the marvels
she has seen in distant Italy.

Be Still My Heart

Within my heart sleeps a lion, needful to be fed,
alongside the lamb sacrificed, which has been bled.
Sprinkled over the fire of life, the sweet fat,
to sputter and burn without the vat,
the sweet aroma of a lamb's forth giving
issues to heaven the spirit of the living.

The fire burns, the heat bursting life from tinders.
The smoke wafts across glowing cinders.

Within my mind, restless as a hunted roe in the forest,
are thoughts of the morrow and yesterday, in rhyme and in chorus.

Throughout the day of anxious expectations
come visions of nymphs in whirling gyrations.
Like fairies, like butterflies, like bright hummingbirds,
each one carrying phrases of scintillating words.

Oh, restless mind be still, do not be void of spirit.
My angel has departed, I fear it.
Oh, stop your bleating, you silly heart.
Your love's not gone, though we're apart.
Soon your heart will cease its menace
and your love will return from distant Venice.

Until Then

My heart whispers to me of your loveliness,
a soft murmuring of a sweet memory
as I recall the warmth of our sweet breath
and how your smile comforts me.
This wondrous love within my heart
I send with you. We won't be apart
although there are days and miles between our kiss,
we'll have love's eternal fire glowing in our hearts.
While my tender heart is bleating for your touch,
it will be warmed by the flame you have kindled.
When you're not in my arms to fan the fire,
love's burning ember has never dwindled.
The warmth of your flame rises higher.
My darling, I miss you so much, I aspire.
Each passing day without you near
heightens my love and dedication, dear.
Though you're not beside me in my need,
I feel so much your presence.
Godspeed.
Until that special day when you return,
until your in my arms again,
this flame you have started will glow and burn
to keep me warm until then.

Love in a Well

A well has been dug in a far remote place
by a traveler in time who crossed a vast space.
He knew the water was there, though hidden so deep.
Now it can be dipped for those who yet sleep
to awaken all those who slumber in rest.
It's refreshing and soothing, sustaining at best.
For the embrangled in toils, hardships, and doubt,
just dip in the well, draw the water out.
Drink in earnest of every drop imbuing,
inhale the elixir—taken in quantity, it's renewing.
I saw you at the well to bring up its nectar.
We were two venturers in time with a common vector
seeking and searching through this wide world over
until this time at this well we'd discover
the effervescence of unrequited love unbounded
whence before the drifting dunes of desires only confounded.
But lo, the well of life is not a mirage or apparition.
So forge straight ahead in spite of attrition.
As so many before have found this well of life
washes away doubts and fears, even strife,
so drink deeply as others have, you're entreated.
In the passage of time this admonishment is repeated.
Now this philosopher's words are meant to impart
treasures immeasurable and reveal mysteries of heart.
Peruse these words I've written today.
Search their meaning—what do they say?
The extent of my wisdom is not of my own
for wisdom itself has riches to be sown
to others who share the cup that you dip.
Each swallow a joy, drink heartily, and don't sip.
There is love for all in the well of life.

Love's Longing

The hour glass is nigh empty,
the sand nearly sifted through.
These lonesome days too plenty,
these nights I've longed for you.
When the sweet morn awakens me
to find you're not by my side,
all the singing of the song birds
cannot my pining hide.
Oh, how dark the midnight hour,
knowing the hunger day will bring.
My sweet angel, my flower
is yet not here,
my heart, oh how it does sting.
Angel, you are my eternal desire,
my sweet well, my precious trove.
Though cool mountain streams I've tasted,
I'm refreshed only by drinking your love.
Fill my cup, let not a drop be wasted,
your elixir sustains me in my emptiness.
Until that long awaited hour of your return
when I taste again of your loveliness,
my impatient waiting, my panting heart,
anticipates your warmth, your consoling touch.
This burning hot coal of love never fading,
this fire within will not part.
But yet just a little while
will I yearn so much,
for soon shall you return to me
in your glorious way we'll touch,
then with you beside me
will I be happy
and my aching heart set free.

Dreams Come True

You say there is another that we'll have to part
but that will never smother the love in my heart.
When you said farewell I well understood the reason.
This love in my heart wasn't planted for a season.
The budding, the blooming blossomed for eternity,
the fragrance and hue is a treasure for me,
a treasure to keep so deep in my soul,
where it will rest forever after the bells toll.
You have unlocked the gates, rolled back the stone.
Every corner of my heart I have fully shown.
With tender eagerness I've relished our love.
You have adorned my heart like a phantom dove.
No tears need be shed, no sighs, no remorse.
I have only precious memories from love's resource.
As the phoenix rises toward sun,
my heart has been lifted by you. You're the one,
the one who has ordained my desire within,
the one who encouraged me so I could begin
to find deeper treasures in life's hidden places.
After searching many times and missing so many faces,
my forgotten fantasies of finding an angel like you
have become a reality—
I know dreams come true.

Paradise Gained

Because your loving spirit peered into my heart,
seeking my innermost soul,
in whole, not in part,
I am compelled, I am laid upon.
I am naked to reveal,
to fully expose how I am taken
by your image of feminine perfection.
Your warm and caring heart,
of graceful inflection
now has my heart, my soul, my spirit,
my very being.
It is healing, it is feeling, it is reeling
in a vortex fleeing from earthly ties.
The skies are no longer cloudy or gray.
Like the moon which is not seen in the light of day,
the essence of your being has permeated to my marrow.
You have left no room in my heart for sorrow.
I am immersed in all that you are to me,
all that I would hope or dream you to be.
More than I thought ever could be,
I am fully absorbed in your beauty.

You have brought me closer to paradise
than any man breathing should be.
Because of your loving spirit,
because of your heavenly aura
with its mystic flow,
I am filled with sunshine and a soft moon glow.
All that you are has entered my heart unseen.
Just as the moon influences the tide,
you draw me to your shores.
Just as the moon, you carry me afar
to the outer depths of an endless sea.
Your love and emotions which were before unknown to me,
now I know.
Paradise is not beyond the sunset.
It is not unattainable
It's not a fantasy,
for I know now how you have given to me
your imbuing love.
I have found paradise with you,
for you have poured your love unto me.

Since I Found You

I found contentment when I found you.
I found an abundance of pleasure so new.
I found you captivating,
a vision of delight to see.
I found in your aplomb
effervescent felicity.
I found what I longed for—
now my searching is through.
My life now has purpose
with a resolve I never knew.
You have led me gently without a command.
Your loveliness is inspiring
with just the touch of your hand.
To be in your arms, I'm desirous
now fully to know love's wonderfulness.
Truly, I'm enraptured by your caress.
Can you see how you have enslaved me?
I abide in rapture for what is to be.
I am satisfied in knowing your love so true.
I savor each moment, each passing hour with you.
You are an angel sent from heaven above,
refreshing as a sun shower, it is you I love.
Yes, I have found love and felicity too,
and tenderness and sweetness
in your eyes so blue.
I have found true love without a doubt.
I have found what complaisance is all about
since I have found you.

Forgive Me

It's all your fault, you see,
because your intoxicating kiss
and your inebriating bliss
has such an influence on me,
an old imbiber such as this.

Forgive me.
I'm in a stupor because you're super.
Just the thought of you makes me dizzy.
I'm reeling and kneeling and feeling,
I need you.
Forgive me.
This old bloke loves to soak
in your love.

Women's Wisdom

When a woman knows that beauty within her heart dwells,
to her it's not a duty.
Her enchantments cast their spells.
For those who understand the enticement of caring,
know that it's not planned, the kindness and sharing.
A mother's tender cradling of a child to her breast,
a sister's gentle counseling when little brother is stressed,
a wife's compassionate nudging when her man is hard pressed,
always with a heart filled with love expressed.
To a woman it is obvious, "in gentleness there is strength."
A man whose strength is gentle is admired at length.
So how does this imbue wisdom to you and me?
It's already in our hearts for each of us to see.

Ask of Me

Ask of me all that you desire,
For your love I so aspire,
entranced by your smiling eyes
and golden hair.
You are the fairest of the fair.
Search my soul and you will find
a relinquished heart,
a dedicated mind.
I seek always you to please.
I would swim across the seven seas
if you but ask it of me.
Touch me with your hands of fire.
Your soft lips take me higher
than eagles soaring on summer zephyrs.
Upward toward heaven so close
my love for you is endlessly rising.
Our thoughts, our feelings are harmonizing.
So transfixed am I in your embrace
by your tender heart so full of grace,
need you ask of me?

Angel

As the shadows lengthen
while the sun descends
and clouds darken,
and the moon begins
its ascension to cast
its soft glow,
I think of you, and I know
this life has meaning,
this life has rewards.
This life will not pass,
it's directed toward
the happiness and fulfillment
each soul seeks with reverence.
Now we know the completeness of love
through perseverance.
I love you.

A poem you request,
for your birthday no less.
I'll do my best too.
Please don't command me, dear,
to do something I fear
such as depart—for that
I have no heart.

Through the Years

Tender thoughts of loveliness,
loving thoughts of tenderness,
sweet memories of each caress,
I'm so in love in our happiness.
You are my angel, and I guess
there is no other to compare.
If there were, I wouldn't care.
In our embrace together we share
love and devotion, for some so rare.
You came to me with enchantress charms,
helpless was I, enfolded in your arms.
I am overtaken by your allure.
I am love struck,
I must adjure.
The passing of time, the waning years
Have never been salted with regretful tears.
We found ourselves smitten with Cupid's spears.
Our love never faint,
absent of fears.
For our love is endless
through the years.

Longing

I am yours, dear angel.
Your soft voice I hear constantly
telling me of enduring love
and your trusting faith in me.

So I long to be in your arms,
always in close harmony.
Do you know your endearing charms
have made a slave of me?

I only live to love you
and to be near you is divine.
I look to your steadfast beauty—
my will is yours,
no longer is it mine.

My heart beats for that hour
in which before you I might be
to inhale of you as a fragrant flower
and draw you close to me.

The depth of my love for you, darling,
is more than I can measure.
For I know wholly fixed in your heart
is love, God's gift, God's treasure.

So I seek always to draw near
your flame of love, as a moth
attracted by your love, warm and tender,
with all its brightness shining forth.

CPSIA information can be obtained at www.ICGtesting.com
Printed in the USA
BVOW07s1140090714

358582BV00002B/91/P